THE BOOK OF
ANCIENT
WISDOM

THE BOOK OF
ANCIENT WISDOM

Over 500 Inspiring Quotations
from the Greeks and Romans

EDITED BY
BILL BRADFIELD

DOVER PUBLICATIONS, INC.
Mineola, New York

Bibliographical Note

The Book of Ancient Wisdom: Over 500 Inspiring Quotations from the Greeks and Romans is a new work, first published by Dover Publications, Inc., in 2005.

Library of Congress Cataloging-in-Publication Data

The book of ancient wisdom : over 500 inspiring quotations from the Greeks and Romans / edited by Bill Bradfield.
    p. cm.
  ISBN-13: 978-0-486-44111-5
  ISBN-10: 0-486-44111-3
    1. Quotations, Latin—Translations into English. 2. Quotations, Greek—Translations into English. I. Bradfield, Bill, 1927–

PN6080.B65 2005
082—dc22

2005041332

Manufactured in the United States by Courier Corporation
44111302   2013
www.doverpublications.com

Quotations by Subject

About the Author

BILL BRADFIELD, compiler and editor of *The Book of Ancient Wisdom,* learned the power of informative, insightful, accurate quotations while working as a reporter early in his journalistic career in Texas. He was editor of award-winning daily and weekly suburban newspapers in the Dallas area and later published *Financial Trend: The Newsweekly of South-western Industry and Investments* in the 1970s and '80s. Bill and his wife, Clare, have collaborated on three books about Texas towns. They live in Dallas.

ADVERSITY

If all our misfortunes were laid in one common heap whence everyone must take an equal portion, most people would be contented to take their own and depart.

        ~ SOCRATES

Adversity reveals genius, prosperity conceals it.

        ~ HORACE

No tree becomes rooted and sturdy unless many a wind assails it. For by its very tossing it tightens its grip and plants its roots more securely. The fragile trees are those that have grown in a sunny valley.

        ~ SENECA

Nothing happens to anybody which he is not fitted by nature to bear.

        ~ MARCUS AURELIUS

In victory even the cowardly like to boast, while in adverse times even the brave are discredited.

        ~ SALLUST

Brave men rejoice in adversity, just as brave soldiers triumph in war.

        ~ SENECA

There is in the worst of fortune the best of chances for a happy change.

~ EURIPIDES

Anyone can hold the helm when the sea is calm.

~ PUBLILIUS SYRUS

Nothing is miserable unless you think it so.

~ BOETHIUS

On the occasion of every accident that befalls you . . . inquire what power you have for turning it to use.

~ EPICTETUS

Time bears away all things.

~ VIRGIL

Human misery must somewhere have a stop. There is no wind that always blows a storm.

~ EURIPIDES

We often give our enemies the means for our own destruction.

~ AESOP

Who except the gods can live time through forever without any pain?

~ AESCHYLUS

Remember that there is nothing stable in human affairs. Therefore avoid undue elation in prosperity or undue depression in adversity.

~ ISOCRATES

Adversity has the effect of eliciting talents which in prosperous circumstances would have been dormant.

~ HORACE

It is difficulties that show what men are.

~ EPICTETUS

Yield thou not to adversity, but press on the more bravely.

~ VIRGIL

If there were no tribulation, there would be no rest. If there were no winter, there would be no summer.

~ SAINT JOHN CHRYSOSTOM

Fire is the test of gold, adversity of strong men.

~ SENECA

Friendship makes prosperity more brilliant, and lightens adversity by dividing and sharing it.

~ CICERO

In prosperity friends do not leave you unless it's desired, whereas in adversity they stay away of their own accord.

~ DEMETRIUS

From their errors and mistakes, the wise and good learn wisdom for the future.

~ PLUTARCH

The good things that belong to prosperity are to be wished, but the good things that belong to adversity are to be admired.

~ SENECA

With man, most of his misfortunes are occasioned by man.

~ PLINY THE ELDER

Learn to see in another's calamity the ills which you should avoid.

~ PUBLILIUS SYRUS

It is a painful thing to look at your own trouble and know that you yourself and no one else has made it.

~ SOPHOCLES

The beauty of the soul shines out when a man bears with composure one heavy mischance after another, not because he does not feel them, but because he is a man of high and heroic temper.

~ ARISTOTLE

ART AND ARTISTS

Art is in love with luck, and luck with art.

~ AGATHON

All art is but imitation of nature.

~ SENECA THE ELDER

As to the artists, do we not know that he only of them whom love inspires has the light of fame? He whom love touches not walks in darkness.

~ PLATO

To be instructed in the arts softens the manners and makes men gentle.

~ OVID

That which achieves its effect by accident is not art.

~ SENECA

Poverty is the discoverer of all the arts.

~ APULEIUS

Art is man's refuge from adversity.

~ MENANDER

Bill Bradfield

A picture is a poem without words.

∼ HORACE

The aim of art is not the outward appearance of things but their inner significance.

∼ ARISTOTLE

BEAUTY

Personal beauty is a greater recommendation than any letter of reference.

               ~ ARISTOTLE

Beauty is a short-lived tyranny.

               ~ SOCRATES

When a girl ceases to blush, she has lost the most powerful charm of her beauty.

         ~ GREGORY I, THE GREAT

Beauty of style and harmony and grace and good rhythm depend upon simplicity.

               ~ PLATO

Judgment of beauty can err, what with the wine and the dark.

               ~ OVID

Anything in any way beautiful derives its beauty from itself, and asks nothing beyond itself. Praise is no part of it, for nothing is made worse or better by praise.

         ~ MARCUS AURELIUS

I know a man who, when he saw a woman of striking beauty, praised the Creator for her. The sight of her lit within him the love of God.

~ Saint John Climacus

Beauty is indeed a good gift of God. But that the good may not think it a great good, God dispenses it even to the wicked.

~ Saint Augustine of Hippo

I pray, O God, that I may be beautiful within.

~ Socrates

What is beautiful is good, and who is good will soon also be beautiful.

~ Sappho of Lesbos

Beauty is a gift of God.

~ Aristotle

Nothing's beautiful from every point of view.

~ Horace

When the candles are out, all women are fair.

~ Plutarch

BOOKS AND LIBRARIES

It does not matter how many books you have, but
whether they are good or not.

> ∾ SENECA

The book you are reading has some good things, some
indifferent, and many bad. There's no other way, Avitus,
to make a book.

> ∾ MARTIAL

Books are . . . a delight at home, and no hindrance
abroad; companions at night, in travelling, in the country.

> ∾ CICERO

Take up and read, take up and read!

> ∾ SAINT AUGUSTINE OF HIPPO

(Alexander the Great) was naturally a great lover of all
kinds of learning and reading . . . he constantly laid
Homer's *Iliad* . . . with his dagger under his pillow,
declaring that he esteemed it a perfect portable treasure
of all military virtue and knowledge.

> ∾ PLUTARCH

Employ your time in improving yourself by other men's writing, so that you shall come easily by what others have labored hard for.

            ∽ SOCRATES

He (Pliny the Elder) used to say that "no book was so bad but some good might be got out of it."

            ∽ PLINY THE YOUNGER

A room without books is as a body without a soul.

            ∽ CICERO

Books have their own destiny.

            ∽ TERENTIANUS MAURUS

CONTENTMENT

Do not spoil what you have by desiring what you have not, but remember that what you have now was once among the things only hoped for.

~ EPICURUS

Well-being is attained little by little, and is no small thing itself.

~ ZENO OF CITIUM

Be content with your lot; one cannot be first in everything.

~ AESOP

The sixth step of humility is to be content in all things. We are to be content with the meanest and worst of everything. In all things we must be mindful of our own lowliness, considering ourselves to be lowly and meek, knowing that though we have nothing in this life, the Lord is always present with us.

~ SAINT BENEDICT OF NURSIA

The best of blessings: a contented mind.

~ HORACE

He is a man of sense who does not grieve for what he has not, but rejoices in what he has.

~ EPICTETUS

Take full account of the excellencies which you possess, and in gratitude remember how you would hanker after them, if you had them not.

~ MARCUS AURELIUS

COURAGE

Danger gleams like sunshine to a brave man's eyes.

~ EURIPIDES

Courage makes men perform noble acts in the midst of danger according to the dictates of the law and in submission to it; the contrary is cowardice.

~ ARISTOTLE

Fortune helps the brave.

~ VIRGIL

He is the best man who, when making his plans, fears and reflects on everything that can happen to him, but in the moment of action is bold.

~ HERODOTUS

Courage in danger is half the battle.

~ PLAUTUS

In times of stress be bold and valiant.

~ HOMER

Audacity augments courage; hesitation, fear.

~ PUBLILIUS SYRUS

Fortune and love favor the brave.

~ OVID

Let us be brave in the face of adversity.

~ SENECA

Blessings on your young courage, boy. That's the way to the stars.

~ VIRGIL

He shall fare well who confronts circumstances aright.

~ PLUTARCH

It is easy to be brave from a safe distance.

~ AESOP

It is courage, courage, courage, that raises the blood of life to crimson splendor. Live bravely and present a brave front to adversity!

~ HORACE

Courage is to take hard knocks like a man when occasion calls.

~ PLAUTUS

Happy the man who ventures boldly to defend what he holds dear.

~ OVID

There is nothing in the world so much admired as a man who knows how to bear unhappiness with courage.

~ SENECA

To persevere, trusting in what he hopes he has, is
courage. The coward despairs.

~ EURIPIDES

Sometimes even to live is an act of courage.

~ SENECA

Nothing is as valuable to a man as courage.

~ TERENCE

Those who cannot bravely face danger are the slaves of
their attackers.

~ ARISTOTLE

Just as one man's body is naturally stronger than
another's for labor, so one man's soul is naturally braver
than another's in danger.

~ SOCRATES

The bravest are surely those who have the clearest
vision of what is before them, glory and danger alike, and
yet notwithstanding, go out to meet it.

~ THUCYDIDES

God himself favors the brave.

~ OVID

Courage is what preserves our liberty, safety, life, and
our homes and parents, our country and children.
Courage comprises all things.

~ PLAUTUS

Bill Bradfield

Being a man, ne'er ask the gods for a life set free from grief, but ask for courage that endureth long.

~ MENANDER

Courage easily finds its own eloquence.

~ PLAUTUS

Courage is a kind of salvation.

~ PLATO

Courage is the virtue that champions the cause of right.

~ CICERO

DEATH

When a man dies, all his glory among men dies also.

~ STESICHORUS

Go tell the Spartans, thou that passeth by
That here, obedient to their laws, we lie.

~ SIMONIDES OF CEOS (epitaph)

It is enough to have perished once.

~ VIRGIL

Not lost, but gone before.

~ PUBLILIUS SYRUS

A dead man cannot bite.

~ PLUTARCH

The fear of death is indeed the pretense of wisdom, and not real wisdom, being a pretense of knowing the unknown; and no one knows whether death, which men in their fear apprehend to be the greatest evil, may not be the greatest good.

~ PLATO

That day, which you fear as being the end of all things, is the birthday of your eternity.

~ SENECA

What is death at most? It is a journey for a season, a sleep longer than usual. If thou fearest death, thou shouldest also fear sleep.

~ SAINT JOHN CHRYSOSTOM

It is God's law, that as things rose so they should fall, as they waxed so should grow old, the strong become weak, and the great become little, and when they become weak and little, they end.

~ SAINT CYPRIAN

By the death of One the world was redeemed . . . We prove by this divine example that death alone found immortality and that death redeemed itself.

~ SAINT AMBROSE

And as for death, if there be any gods, it is no grievous thing to leave the society of men. The gods will do thee no hurt, thou mayest be sure. But if it be so that there be no gods, or that they take no care of the world, why should I desire to live in a world void of gods and of all divine providence?

~ MARCUS AURELIUS

The life of the dead consists in being present in the minds of the living.

~ CICERO

The house of mourning teaches charity and wisdom.

~ SAINT JOHN CHRYSOSTOM

The act of dying is also one of the acts of life.

∼ MARCUS AURELIUS

Whom the gods love dies young.

∼ MENANDER

If I err in my belief that the souls of men are immortal, I err gladly and do not wish to lose so delightful an error.

∼ CICERO

These passions of soul, these conflicts so fierce, will cease, and be repressed by the casting of a little dust.

∼ VIRGIL

Be of good cheer about death, and know this of a truth: no evil can happen to a good man, either in life or after death.

∼ SOCRATES

If fame comes after death, I'm in no hurry for it.

∼ MARTIAL

EDUCATION

Above all things we must take care that the child, who is not yet old enough to love his studies, does not come to hate them and dread the bitterness which he has once tasted, even when the years of infancy are left behind. His studies must be made an amusement.

~ QUINTILIAN

He who seeks knowledge must desire from a young age to hear the entire truth.

~ PLATO

Knowledge which is acquired under compulsion has no hold on the mind. Therefore do not use compulsion, but let early education be rather a sort of amusement. This will better enable you to find out the natural bent of the child.

~ PLATO

Education is a controlling grace to the young, consolation to the old, wealth to the poor, and contentment to the rich.

~ DIOGENES OF SINOPE

Nature without learning is blind; learning apart from nature is fractional, and practice in the absence of both is useless.

~ PLUTARCH

Only the educated are free.

~ EPICTETUS

Whoso neglects learning in his youth, loses the past and is dead for the future.

~ EURIPIDES

It is only the ignorant who despise education.

~ PUBLILIUS SYRUS

The direction in which education starts a man will determine his future life.

~ PLATO

He who influences the thought of his times, influences all of the times that follow. He has made his impress on eternity.

~ HYPATIA OF ALEXANDRIA

Much learning does not teach understanding.

~ HERACLITIS

Education is an ornament in prosperity and a refuge in adversity.

~ ARISTOTLE

And seek for truth in the groves of Academe.

~ HORACE

I grow old learning something new every day.

~ SOLON

I swear . . . to hold my teacher in this art equal to my own parents; to make him partner in my livelihood; when he is in need of money to share mine with him; to consider his family as my own brothers and to teach them this art if they want to learn it, without fee or indenture.

~ HIPPOCRATES (Hippocratic Oath)

To become self-educated, you should condemn yourself for all those things you would criticize others.

~ DIOGENES OF SINOPE

From all wild beasts, a child is the most difficult to handle.

~ PLATO

We must remember that one man is much the same as another, and that he is best who is trained in the severest school.

~ THUCYDIDES

If we don't mold clay, it does not become a ceramic.

~ XENOPHON

It is impossible for a man to learn what he thinks he already knows.

~ EPICTETUS

It does not make much difference what a person studies—all knowledge is related, and the man who studies anything, if he keeps at it, will become learned.

~ HYPATIA OF ALEXANDRIA

ENVY

Potter bears a grudge against potter, and craftsman against craftsman, and beggar is envious of beggar, the bard of bard.

~ HESIOD

We are all clever enough at envying a famous man while he is yet alive, and at praising him when he is dead.

~ MIMNERMUS OF COLOPHON

Envy, the meanest of vices, creeps on the ground like a serpent.

~ OVID

I am sure the grapes are sour.

~ AESOP

In few men is it part of nature to respect a friend's prosperity without begrudging him.

~ AESCHYLUS

Our nature holds so much envy and malice that our pleasure in our own advantages is not so great as our distress at others'.

~ PLUTARCH

How much better a thing it is to be envied rather than pitied.

~ HERODOTUS

He who goes unenvied shall not be admired.

~ AESCHYLUS

From envy are born hatred, detraction, calumny, joy caused by the misfortune of a neighbor, and displeasure caused by his prosperity.

~ GREGORY I, THE GREAT

(Envy is) the diabolical sin.

~ SAINT AUGUSTINE OF HIPPO

The vulgar bark at men of mark, as dogs bark at strangers.

~ SENECA

Do not envy the wealth of your neighbor.

~ HOMER

As iron is eaten away by rust, so the envious are consumed by their own passion.

~ ANTISTHENES

Even success softens not the heart of the envious.

~ PINDAR

The man who covets is always poor.

~ CLAUDIAN

FORGIVENESS

Bear and forbear.

~ OVID

Forgiveness is better than revenge.

~ PITTACUS OF MITYLENE

It is right for him who asks forgiveness for his offenses to grant it to others.

~ HORACE

I can pardon everyone's mistakes but my own.

~ CATO THE ELDER

If we entreat God that he would forgive us, we also ought to forgive, for we are before the eyes of our Lord and God.

~ SAINT POLYCARP

FRIENDSHIP

Nothing will ever please me, no matter how excellent or beneficial, if I must retain the knowledge of it to myself. No good thing is pleasant to possess without friends to share it.

        ~ SENECA

What is a friend? A single soul dwelling in two bodies.

        ~ ARISTOTLE

Be slow to fall into friendship, but when thou art in, continue firm and constant.

        ~ SOCRATES

True friends visit us in prosperity only when invited, but in adversity they come without invitation.

        ~ THEOPHRASTUS

It is not so much our friends' help that helps us as the confident knowledge that they will help us.

        ~ EPICURUS

A true friend is a sort of second self.

        ~ CICERO

Friends are much better tried in bad fortune than in good.

~ ARISTOTLE

We should render a service to a friend to bind him closer to us, and to an enemy in order to make a friend out of him.

~ CLEOBULUS

Every man, however wise, needs the advice of some sagacious friend in the affairs of life.

~ PLAUTUS

You will best serve your friends if you do not wait for them to ask your help but go of your own accord at the crucial moment to lend them aid.

~ ISOCRATES

Don't ask of your friends what you yourself can do.

~ ENNIUS

Friendship is equality.

~ ARISTOTLE

I would prefer as a friend a good man who is ignorant than one more clever who is evil, too.

~ EURIPIDES

Sharing is a token of friendship. One does not want to share even a journey with one's enemies.

~ ARISTOTLE

Choose for thy friend, the friend of virtue. Yield to his gentle counsel, profit by his life, and for a trifling grievance never leave him.

~ PYTHAGORAS

Make no man your friend before inquiring how he has used his former friends, for you must expect him to treat you as he has treated them. Be slow to give your friendship, but when you have given it, strive to make it lasting; it is as reprehensible to make many changes in one's associates as to have no friend at all.

~ ISOCRATES

You win the victory when you yield to friends.

~ SOPHOCLES

If two friends ask you to judge a dispute, don't accept, because you will lose one friend. On the other hand, if two strangers come with the same request, accept, because you will gain one friend.

~ SAINT AUGUSTINE OF HIPPO

Since we are mortal, friendships are best kept to a moderate level, rather than sharing the very depths of our souls.

~ SAINT HIPPOLYTUS

It is characteristic of good men neither to go wrong themselves nor to allow their friends to do so.

~ ARISTOTLE

The base honor their friends only when they are present; the good cherish their friends even when they are far away. While it takes only a short time to break up

the intimacies of the base, not all eternity can blot out
the friendship of good men.

~ ISOCRATES

Man's best support is a very dear friend.

~ CICERO

Friends are an aid to the young to guard them from
error; to the elderly, to attend to their wants and to
supplement their failing power of action; to those in the
prime of life to assist them in noble deeds.

~ ARISTOTLE

Unless you bear with the faults of a friend, you betray
your own.

~ PUBLILIUS SYRUS

We should behave to our friends as we would wish our
friends to behave to us.

~ ARISTOTLE

There are limits to the indulgence which friendship
allows.

~ CICERO

There are only two people who can tell you the truth
about yourself: an enemy who has lost his temper, and a
friend who loves you dearly.

~ ANTISTHENES

Forget your woes when you see your friends.

~ PRISCIAN

It is a good thing to be rich, it is a good thing to be strong, but it is a better thing to be beloved of many friends.

                                        ~ EURIPIDES

Friendship makes prosperity more brilliant, and lightens adversity by dividing and sharing it.

                                            ~ CICERO

Rather throw away that which is dearest to you, your own life, than turn away a good friend.

                                        ~ SOPHOCLES

One who's our friend is fond of us. One who's fond of us isn't necessarily our friend.

                                           ~ SENECA

Wishing to be friends is quick work, but friendship is a slow-ripening fruit.

                                         ~ ARISTOTLE

To like and dislike the same things, this is what makes a solid friendship.

                                           ~ SALLUST

Life has no blessing like a prudent friend.

                                          ~ EURIPIDES

Great grace may go with a little gift, and precious are all things that come from friends.

                                          ~ THEOCRITUS

The Romans assisted their allies and friends, and acquired friendships by giving rather than receiving kindness.

∼ SALLUST

Friends are as companions on a journey, who ought to aid each other to persevere on the road to a happier life.

∼ PYTHAGORAS

I don't need a friend who changes when I change and who nods when I nod. My shadow does that much better.

∼ PLUTARCH

GENEROSITY

We should give as we would receive—cheerfully, quickly, and without hesitation, for there is no grace in a benefit that sticks to the fingers.

~ SENECA

Leave the field if thou art victorious; it is noble to spare the vanquished.

~ STATIUS

He who confers a favor should at once forget it, if he is not to show a sordid ungenerous spirit. To remind a man of a kindess conferred and to talk of it, is little different from reproach.

~ DEMOSTHENES

You may send poetry to the rich; to poor men, give substantial presents.

~ MARTIAL

Get not your friends by bare compliments, but by giving them sensible tokens of your love.

~ SOCRATES

GRATITUDE AND THANKFULNESS

He who receives a benefit with gratitude repays the first installment on his debt.

~ SENECA

A thankful heart is not only the greatest virtue, but the parent of all other virtues.

~ CICERO

From everything that happens in the universe, it is easy for a man to find occasion to praise providence if he has within himself these two qualities: the faculty of taking a comprehensive view of what has happened in each individual instance, and the sense of gratitude.

~ EPICTETUS

Men are slower to recognize blessings than evils.

~ LIVY

He that urges gratitude pleads the cause both of God and men, for without it we can be neither sociable or religious.

~ SENECA

No duty is more urgent than that of returning thanks.

~ SAINT AMBROSE

A man can refrain from wanting what he has not, and cheerfully make the best of a bird in the hand.

~ SENECA

GREED AND GLUTTONY

The covetous man is ever in want.

∼ HORACE

The most grievous kind of destitution is to need money in the midst of wealth.

∼ SENECA

The miser is as much in want of what he has as what he has not.

∼ PUBLILIUS SYRUS

Thinking to get at once all the gold the goose could give, he killed it, and opened it only to find: nothing.

∼ AESOP

Greed's worst point is its ingratitude.

∼ SENECA

Whoever does not regard what he has as most ample wealth is unhappy, though he is master of the world.

∼ EPICURUS

Poverty is in want of much, but avarice of everything.

∼ PUBLILIUS SYRUS

Majestic, mighty wealth is the holiest of our gods.

~ JUVENAL

I could not possibly count the gold-digging ruses of women. Not if I had ten mouths, not if I had ten months.

~ OVID

Nothing is more intolerable than a wealthy woman.

~ JUVENAL

It is for the superfluous things of life that men sweat.

~ SENECA

He is bound fast by his wealth . . . His money owns him rather than he owns it.

~ SAINT CYPRIAN

Riches that are the fruit of dishonest labor are full of shame.

~ DEMOCRITUS

Luxury and avarice have similar results.

~ MENANDER

In a rich man's house there is no place to spit but in his face.

~ DIOGENES OF SINOPE

Acorns were good enough until bread was invented.

~ JUVENAL

You think that I am cruel and gluttonous when I beat my cook for sending in a bad dinner. But if that is too trivial a cause, what other can there be for beating a cook?

~ MARTIAL

Wine leads to folly. It makes even the wisest laugh too much. It makes him dance. It makes him say what should have been left unsaid.

~ HOMER

What does drunkenness not accomplish? It unlocks secrets, confirms our hopes, urges the indolent into battle, lifts the burden from anxious minds, teaches new arts.

~ HORACE

The company of just and righteous men is better than wealth and a rich estate.

~ EURIPIDES

Avarice is a cursed vice. Offer a man enough gold and he will part with his own small hoard of food, however great his hunger.

~ LUCAN

HAPPINESS

True happiness consists in being considered deserving of it.

~ PLINY THE ELDER

No one is happy all his life long.

~ EURIPIDES

There is only one way to happiness and that is to cease worrying about things which are beyond the power of our will.

~ EPICTETUS

To live happily is an inward power of the soul.

~ MARCUS AURELIUS

Our happiness depends upon wisdom all the way.

~ SOPHOCLES

All seek joy, but it is not found on earth.

~ SAINT JOHN CHRYSOSTOM

Call no man happy until he dies; he is at best fortunate.

~ SOLON

Where your pleasure is, there is your treasure; where your treasure, there your heart; where your heart, there your happiness.

~ SAINT AUGUSTINE OF HIPPO

To marvel at nothing is just about the one and only thing, Numicius, that can make a man happy and keep him that way.

~ HORACE

Happiness depends upon ourselves.

~ ARISTOTLE

Not the owner of many possessions will you be right to call happy. He more rightly deserves the name of happy who knows how to use the gods' gifts wisely and to put up with rough poverty, and who fears dishonor more than death.

~ HORACE

When a man has lost all happiness, he's not alive. Call him a breathing corpse.

~ SOPHOCLES

The essence of philosophy is that a man should so live that his happiness shall depend as little as possible on external things.

~ EPICTETUS

Happiness is the meaning and purpose of life, the whole aim and end of human existence.

~ ARISTOTLE

If thou workest at that which is before thee . . . expecting nothing, fearing nothing, but satisfied with thy present activity according to Nature, and with heroic truth in every word and sound which thou utterest, thou wilt live happy. And there is no man who is able to prevent this.

~ MARCUS AURELIUS

Happy is the man who ventures boldly to defend what he holds dear.

~ OVID

We deem those happy who from the experience of life have learned to bear its ills, without being overcome by them.

~ JUVENAL

Happiness is an expression of the soul in considered actions.

~ ARISTOTLE

The happiness of your mind depends upon the quality of your thoughts.

~ SENECA

No man is happy unless he believes he is.

~ PUBLILIUS SYRUS

It is in virtue that happiness consists, for virtue is the state of mind which tends to make the whole of life harmonious.

~ ZENO OF CITIUM

And may I live the remainder of my life . . . for myself, may there be plenty of books and many years' more of the fruits of the earth!

~ HORACE

For in every ill-turn of fortune the most unhappy sort of misfortune is to have been happy.

                   ∾ BOETHIUS

No man can live happily who regards himself alone, who turns everything to his own advantage. Thou must live for another if thou wishest to live for thyself.

                   ∾ SENECA

That man is happiest who lives from day to day and asks no more, garnering the simple goodness of a life.

                   ∾ EURIPIDES

We rich men count our happiness to lie in the little superfluities, not in necessities.

                   ∾ PLUTARCH

Happy is he who could learn the causes of all things and who put beneath his feet all fears.

                   ∾ VIRGIL

One swallow does not make a summer; neither does one day. Similarly, neither can one day, or a brief space of time, make a man blessed and happy.

                   ∾ ARISTOTLE

A wise man sings his joy in the closet of his heart.

                   ∾ TIBULLUS

HASTE

To do two things at once is to do neither.

       ~ PUBLILIUS SYRUS

Hasten deliberately.

       ~ OCTAVIAN AUGUSTUS CAESAR

Nothing can be done at once hastily and prudently.

       ~ PUBLILIUS SYRUS

Every delay, however trifling, seems too long for a man in haste.

       ~ SENECA

Nothing is seen clearly and certainly by a man in a hurry. Haste is improvident and blind.

       ~ LIVY

He finishes too late who goes too fast.

       ~ PUBLILIUS SYRUS

Make haste slowly.

       ~ OCTAVIAN AUGUSTUS CAESAR

THE HEAVENS

Man gazes at the stars, but his feet are in the mud.

⟿ SENECA

. . . he passed far beyond the flaming walls of the world and traversed throughout in mind and spirit the immeasurable universe.

⟿ LUCRETIUS

Look 'round at the courses of the stars, as if thou were going along with them; and constantly consider the changes of the elements into one another; for such thoughts purge away the filth of the terrene life.

⟿ MARCUS AURELIUS

I know that I am mortal and ephemeral. But when I search for the close-knit encompassing convolutions of the stars, my feet no longer touch the earth, but in the presence of Zeus himself I take my fill of ambrosia which the gods produce.

⟿ SAINT POLYCARP

The sun comes into being each day from little pieces of fire that are collected.

⟿ XENOPHANES

Vain would be the attempt of telling all the figures of
the stars circling as in a dance, and their juxtapositions,
and the return of them in their revolutions upon
themselves, and their approximations.

~ PLATO

No man is utterly dull and obtuse, with head so bent
on Earth, as never to lift himself up and rise with all his
soul to the contemplation of the starry heavens, especially
when some fresh wonder shows a beacon-light in the sky.
As long as the ordinary course of heaven runs on, custom
robs it of its true size. Such is our constitution that
objects of daily occurence pass unnoticed even when
most worthy of our admiration. On the other hand, the
sight even of trifling things is attractive if their
appearance is unusual. So this concourse of stars, which
paints with beauty the spacious firmament on high,
gathers no concourse of the nation. But when there is any
change in the wonted order, then all eyes are turned to
the sky . . . So natural it is to admire what is strange
rather than what is great.

~ SENECA

And oft, before tempestuous winds arise,
The seeming stars fall headlong from the skies,
And, shooting through the darkness, gild the night
With sweeping glories and long trains of light.

~ VIRGIL

He wrought the earth, the heavens, and the sea;
the moon also at her full and the untiring sun, with all
the signs that glorify the face of heaven—the Pleiads, the
Hyads, huge Orion, and the Bear, which men also call the
Wain and which turns around ever in one place, facing
Orion, and alone never dips into the stream of Oceanus.

~ HOMER

This universe is called Cosmos, or order, not disorder
or misrule.

~ PLATO

If one of these fires of unusual shape has made its
appearance, everybody is eager to know what it is. Blind
to all other celestial bodies, each asks about the
newcomer. One is not quite sure whether to admire or to
fear it. Persons there are who seek to inspire terror by
forecasting its grave import.

~ SENECA

People may injure their bodily eye by observing and
gazing on the sun during an eclipse, unless they take the
precaution of only looking at the image reflected in the
water or in some similar medium.

~ PLATO

By the original composition of the universe, sky and
earth had one form, their natures being mingled, after
this their bodies parted from each other, and the world
took on the whole agreement that we see in it.

~ DIODORUS SICULUS

A day will come in which zealous research over long
periods of time will bring to light things that still now lie
hidden. The life of a single man, even if he devotes it
entirely to the heavens, is insufficient to fathom so broad
a field. Knowledge will thus unfold only over the course
of generations. But there will come a time when our
descendants will marvel that we did not know the things
that seem so simple to them. Many discoveries are
reserved for future centuries, however, when we are long
forgotten. Our universe would be deplorably insignificant

had it not offered every generation new problems.
Nature does not surrender her secrets once and for all.

~ SENECA

The day, water, sun, moon, night: I do not have to
purchase these things with money.

~ PLAUTUS

The world thus shaped then is not at rest but eternally
revolves with indescribable velocity, each revolution
occupying the space of 24 hours. The rising and setting of
the sun have left this not doubtful.

~ PLINY THE ELDER

HOPE

Where there is life, there is hope.

~ TERENCE

The short span of life forbids us to take on far-reaching hopes.

~ HORACE

I am full of hope, but the end lies in God.

~ PINDAR

If you do not hope, you will not find out what is beyond your hopes.

~ SAINT CLEMENT OF ALEXANDRIA

Just as dumb creatures are snared by food, human beings would not be caught unless they had a nibble of hope.

~ PETRONIUS

Hope is a waking dream.

~ ARISTOTLE

JUSTICE

Justice is the earnest and constant will to render every man his due. The precepts of the law are these: to live honorably, to injure no other man, to render to every man his due.

~ JUSTINIAN I

Nothing is to be preferred before justice.

~ SOCRATES

A kingdom founded on injustice never lasts.

~ SENECA

When you act justly, you have the gods for allies.

~ MENANDER

Every virtue is included in the idea of justice, and every just man is good.

~ THEOGNIS

The fundamentals of justice are that no one shall suffer wrong, and that the public good be served.

~ CICERO

Though justice moves slowly, it seldom fails to overtake the wicked.

~ HORACE

Wrong must not win by technicalities.

~ AESCHYLUS

Justice is the crowning glory of the virtues.

~ CICERO

Mankind censures injustice, fearing that they may be victims of it and not because they shrink from committing it.

~ PLATO

More laws, less justice.

~ CICERO

There is no such thing as justice in the abstract. It is merely a compact between men.

~ EPICURUS

If they are just, they are better than clever.

~ SOPHOCLES

Justice . . . is a kind of compact not to harm or be harmed.

~ EPICURUS

How invincible is justice if it be well spoken.

~ CICERO

There are times when even justice brings harm with it.

~ SOPHOCLES

And Heav'n, that ev'ry virtue bears in mind,
Ev'n to the ashes of the just is kind.

∼ HOMER

Into the discussion of human affairs the question of
justice enters only where the pressure of necessity is
equal, and that the powerful exact what they can, and the
weak grant what they must.

∼ THUCYDIDES

The manner by which the masses can see the beauty of
justice is to teach them, by simple means, the results of
injustice.

∼ EURIPIDES

Justice brings much pleasure to the soul because living
without having anything to fear or be ashamed of is a
pleasure and satisfaction in life.

∼ DIOGENES OF SINOPE

An unjust deed doesn't escape the gods' attention.

∼ PLATO

The only time an unjust man will scream against
injustice is when he is afraid someone will practice it
on him.

∼ PLATO

The question of what rules of conduct should govern
the relations between husband and wife, and generally
between friend and friend, seems to be ultimately a
question of justice.

∼ ARISTOTLE

Among all willing injustices, most occur out of greed and ambition.

~ ARISTOTLE

The worse case of injustice is for someone to believe he is just while he is not.

~ PLATO

He hurts the good who spares the bad.

~ PUBLILIUS SYRUS

Only the just man enjoys peace of mind.

~ EPICURUS

All virtue is summed up in dealing justly.

~ ARISTOTLE

KINDNESS

The unfortunate need people who will be kind to them; the prosperous need people to be kind to.

~ ARISTOTLE

One who knows how to show and to accept kindness will be a friend better than any possession.

~ SOPHOCLES

Wherever there is a human being there is a chance for kindness.

~ SENECA

Kindness begets kindness.

~ SOPHOCLES

Let everything be done in moderation. Let the weakness of the old and the very young be always taken into account. Let the weaker be helped so that they may not do their work in sadness.

~ SAINT BENEDICT OF NURSIA

Mercy imitates God and disappoints Satan.

~ SAINT JOHN CHRYSOSTOM

LAW

The good of the people is the supreme law.

~ CICERO

The law is reason free from passion.

~ ARISTOTLE

The purpose of the law is to prevent the strong from always having their way.

~ OVID

Even when laws have been written down, they ought not always to remain unaltered.

~ ARISTOTLE

Law is a pledge that citizens of a state will do justice to one another.

~ LYCOPHRON OF CHALCIS

The people must fight on behalf of the law as though for the city's walls.

~ HERACLITUS

Law is order, and good law is good order.

~ ARISTOTLE

Every king, every despot, is the sworn foe of freedom and of law.

∼ DEMOSTHENES

The more corrupt the state, the more numerous the laws.

∼ TACITUS

Nobody has a more sacred obligation to obey the law than those who make the law.

∼ SOPHOCLES

Rigorous law is often rigorous injustice.

∼ TERENCE

Certain laws have not been written, but they are more fixed than all of the written laws.

∼ SENECA

Good laws, if they are not obeyed, do not constitute good government.

∼ ARISTOTLE

God enjoins what we cannot do, in order that we may know what we have to ask of him.

∼ SAINT AUGUSTINE OF HIPPO

The law was given in order to convert a great into a little man—to show that you have no power of your own for righteousness; and might thus, poor, needy, and destitute, flee to grace.

∼ SAINT AUGUSTINE OF HIPPO

Good people do not need laws to tell them to act responsibly, while bad people will find a way around the laws.

∼ PLATO

No law is quite appropriate for all.

∼ LIVY

LEADERSHIP AND STATESMANSHIP

Reason and judgment are the qualities of a leader.

~ TACITUS

It is frequently a misfortune to have very brilliant men in charge of affairs; they expect too much of ordinary men.

~ THUCYDIDES

He who is a good ruler must have first been ruled.

~ ARISTOTLE

It is impossible to know fully any man's character, will, or judgment, until he has been proved by the test of rule and law-giving.

~ SOPHOCLES

What a great statesman must be most anxious to produce is a certain moral character in his fellow citizens, namely, a disposition to virtue and the performance of virtuous actions.

~ ARISTOTLE

On him who wields power gently, the gods look favorably from afar.

~ AESCHYLUS

There is no greater proof of the abilities of a general than to investigate, with the utmost care, into the character and natural abilities of his opponent.

∽ POLYBIUS

But the actions of those who hold great power, and pass their lives in a lofty status, are known to all men. Therefore, in the highest position there is the least freedom of action.

∽ SALLUST

LOVE

Love is all we have, the only way that each can help the other.

~ EURIPIDES

Love conquers all things. Let us, too, give in to Love.

~ VIRGIL

Who can give law to lovers? Love is a greater law to itself.

~ BOETHIUS

Love blinds all men alike, both the reasonable and the foolish.

~ MENANDER

One word frees us of all the weight and pain of life. That word is love.

~ SOPHOCLES

(Love is) the joy of the good, the wonder of the wise, the amazement of the gods.

~ PLATO

The burden becomes light that is shared by love.

~ OVID

To be beloved, love.

～ AUSONIUS

It is hard for the human soul not to love something.

～ SAINT JEROME

If you wish to be loved, love.

～ SENECA

It is love that asks, that seeks, that knocks, that finds, and that is faithful to what it finds.

～ SAINT AUGUSTINE OF HIPPO

True love can fear no one.

～ SENECA

O love, resistless in thy might, thou triumphest even over gold!

～ SOPHOCLES

All loves should be simply stepping-stones to the love of God. So it was with me; and blest be his name for his great goodness and mercy.

～ PLATO

Love, and do what you like.

～ SAINT AUGUSTINE OF HIPPO

Dignity and love do not blend well, nor do they continue long together.

～ OVID

Lovers remember all things.

～ OVID

The hottest love has the coldest end.

～ SOCRATES

A man can be so changed by love as to be
unrecognizable as the same person.

～ TERENCE

Love, bittersweet and irrepressible, loosens my limbs
and I tremble.

～ SAPPHO OF LESBOS

Love must not touch the marrow of the soul. Our
affections must be breakable chains that we can cast off
or tighten.

～ EURIPIDES

Let those love now, who never loved before. Let those
who have always loved, now love the more.

～ OVID

If a man is in love, he is more daring than cowardly,
and endures many dangers.

～ ARISTOTLE

Your lover is he who loves your soul.

～ SOCRATES

No herb can remedy the anguish of love.

～ OVID

It is only the women of ripe age who understand the
art of love.

～ ARISTOPHANES

Art thou the topmost apple
The gatherers could not reach,
Reddening on the bough?

～ SAPPHO OF LESBOS

The fondness of a lover is not a matter of goodwill but
of appetite which he wishes to satisfy. Just as the wolf
loves the lamb, so the lover adores his beloved.

～ SOCRATES

There is no sort of valor more respected by the gods
than this which comes of love.

～ PLATO

He is no lover who does not love always.

～ ARISTOTLE

It is our care for the helpless, our practice of loving
kindness, that brands us in the eyes of our opponents.
"Look," they say, "how these Christians love one another.
See how they are prepared to die for one another!"

～ TERTULLIAN

I hate and I love. Why I do you may well ask. I do not
know, but I feel it happen and I am in agony.

～ CATULLUS

One word frees us from all the weight and pain of life.
That word is love.

～ SOPHOCLES

The Love-god inflames more fiercely those he sees are
reluctant to surrender.

～ TIBULLUS

LUCK

Chance is always powerful. Let your hook be always cast. In the pool where you least expect it, there will be a fish.

~ OVID

How often things occur by mere chance which we dared not even hope for.

~ TERENCE

'Tis man's to fight, but Heaven's to give success.

~ HOMER

Chance never helps those who do not help themselves.

~ SOPHOCLES

We must master our good fortune or it will master us.

~ PUBLILIUS SYRUS

Fortune reveres the brave, and overwhelms the cowardly.

~ SENECA

No man ever wetted clay and then left it, as if there would be bricks by chance and fortune.

~ PLUTARCH

Fortune sides with him who dares.

~ VIRGIL

Fortune will always confer an aura of worth,
unworthily, and in this world the lucky person passes for
a genius.

~ EURIPIDES

Ah, Fortune, what god is more cruel to us than thou!
How thou delightest to make sport of human life!

~ HORACE

When Fortune flatters, she does it to betray.

~ PUBLILIUS SYRUS

Luck never made a man wise.

~ SENECA

Fortune is not on the side of the faint-hearted.

~ SOPHOCLES

It is easier to get a favor from fortune than to keep it.

~ PUBLILIUS SYRUS

MATHEMATICS AND NUMBERS

There is no royal road to geometry.
~ EUCLID (also attributed to Ptolemy and Menaechmus)

That which, being added to another, does not make it
greater, and being taken away from another, does not
make it less, is nothing.
~ ZENO OF ELEA

Eureka! Eureka! I have found it!
~ ARCHIMEDES (on discovering the principle
of specific gravity)

Falsehood does not inhere in the nature of number
and harmony, for there is no kinship between it and them
. . . Falsehood cannot be breathed into number, being
hostile and inimical to its very nature, whereas truth is
congenial to number and shares close family ties with it.
~ PHILOLAUS OF CROTON

In the discovery of lemmas, the best aid is a mental
aptitude for it.
~ PROCLUS

Bees . . . by virtue of a certain geometrical forethought
. . . know that the hexagon is greater than the square and

the triangle . . . The bees have wisely selected for their
structure that which contains the most angles, suspecting
indeed that it could hold more honey than the other two.

> ∽ PAPPUS OF ALEXANDRIA

Number is the ruler of forms and ideas, and the cause
of gods and demons.

> ∽ PYTHAGORAS

God ever geometrizes.

> ∽ PLATO

There is no smallest among the small and no largest
among the large, but always something still smaller and
something still larger.

> ∽ ANAXAGORAS

He is unworthy of the name of Man who is ignorant of
the fact that the diagonal of a square is incommensurable
with its side.

> ∽ PLATO

There are things that seem incredible to most men
who have not studied mathematics.

> ∽ ARISTOTLE

Numbers rule the universe.

> ∽ PYTHAGORAS

Six is a number perfect in itself, and not because God
created all things in six days. Rather, the inverse is true.
God created all things in six days because the number is
perfect. And it would remain perfect even if the work of
the six days did not exist.

> ∽ SAINT AUGUSTINE OF HIPPO

I have hardly ever known a mathematician who was capable of reasoning.

$\sim$ PLATO

Mathematics is an obscure field, an abtruse science, complicated and exact, yet so many have attained perfection in it that we might conclude almost anyone who seriously applied himself would achieve a measure of success.

$\sim$ CICERO

To Thales, the primary question was not what do we know, but how do we know it?

$\sim$ ARISTOTLE

Willingly would I burn to death like Phaeton, were this the price for reaching the Sun and learning its shape, its size, and its substance.

$\sim$ EUDOXUS OF CNIDUS

Arithmetic has a very great and compelling effect, compelling the soul to reason about abstract number and rebelling against the introduction of visible or intangible objects into the argument.

$\sim$ PLATO

It is evidently equally foolish to accept probable reasoning from a mathematician and to demand from a rhetorician demonstrative proof.

$\sim$ ARISTOTLE

The mind is not a vessel to be filled, it is a fire to be kindled.

$\sim$ PYTHAGORAS

Uneven numbers are the gods' delight.

~ VIRGIL

Why do we believe that in all matters the odd numbers are the more powerful?

~ PLINY THE ELDER

Wherever there is number there is beauty.

~ PROCLUS

But Nature flies from the infinite, for the infinite is unending or imperfect, and Nature ever seeks an end.

~ ARISTOTLE

Objects of sense are not unlimited and therefore the number applying to them cannot be so. Nor is an enumerator able to number to infinity. Although we double, multiply over and over again, we still end with a finite number.

~ PLOTINUS

The so-called Pythagorans, who were the first to take up mathematics, not only advanced this subject, but, having been brought up on it, they thought its principles of mathematics were the principles of all things.

~ ARISTOTLE

He who can properly define and divide is considered a god.

~ PLATO

Infinity is a fathomless gulf, into which all things vanish.

~ MARCUS AURELIUS

Mathematics reminds you of the invisible form of the soul. She gives life to her own discoveries; she awakens the mind and purifies the intellect; she brings light to our intrinsic ideas; she abolishes oblivion and ignorance which are ours by birth.

~ PROCLUS

MIND

The mind is not a vessel to be filled. It is a fire to be kindled.

$\sim$ PLUTARCH

Mind is ever the ruler of the universe.

$\sim$ PLATO

The mind ought sometimes to be amused, that it may better return to thought, and to itself.

$\sim$ PHAEDRUS

Let us train our minds to desire what the situation demands.

$\sim$ SENECA

All paid employments absorb and degrade the mind.

$\sim$ ARISTOTLE

Thou has commanded that an ill-regulated mind should be its own punishment.

$\sim$ SAINT AUGUSTINE OF HIPPO

Choose to have a vigorous mind rather than a vigorous body.

~ Pythagoras

The mind is never right but when it is at peace with itself.

~ Seneca the Elder

MONEY AND PROSPERITY

Money is life to us wretched mortals.

~ HESIOD

Love of money is the disease which makes men most groveling and pitiful.

~ LONGINUS

The image of Caesar is money; the image of God is man. Give money to Caesar and give thyself to God.

~ TERTULLIAN

Money has never yet made anyone rich.

~ SENECA

He who spends rightly acquired fortune in good deeds may never become exceedingly rich, but also he will never be a poor man.

~ PLATO

Nothing that is God's is obtainable by money.

~ TERTULLIAN

Money is to be kept at a distance if one doesn't know how to use it.

~ SOPHOCLES

No one goes to Hades with all his immense wealth.

~ THEOGNIS

Of prosperity mortals can never have enough.

~ AESCHYLUS

The company of just and righteous men is better than wealth and a rich estate.

~ EURIPIDES

Riches are not forbidden, but the pride of them is.

~ SAINT JOHN CHRYSOSTOM

We who are united in mind and soul have no hesitation about sharing property. All is common among us, except our wives.

~ TERTULLIAN

He that hath a penny in his purse is worth a penny. Have and you shall be esteemed.

~ PETRONIUS

The makers of fortunes have a second love of money as a creation of their own, resembling the affection of authors for their own poems, or of parents for their children, beside that natural love of it for the sake of use and profit.

~ PLATO

NATURE

Never does nature say one thing and wisdom another.

~ JUVENAL

Though you drive away nature with a pitchfork, she always returns.

~ HORACE

It is far from easy to determine whether she has proved a kind parent to man or a merciless stepmother.

~ PLINY THE ELDER

It is difficult to change nature.

~ SENECA

Nature loves to hide.

~ HERACLITUS

All that is harmony for thee, O Universe, is in harmony with me as well. Nothing that comes at the right time for thee is too early or too late for me. Everything is fruit to me that thy seasons bring, O Nature. All things come of thee, have their being in thee, and return to thee.

~ MARCUS AURELIUS

No man finds it difficult to return to nature except the man who has deserted nature.

~ SENECA

In all things of nature there is something of the marvelous.

~ ARISTOTLE

Haven't you sometimes seen a cloud that looked like a centaur? Or a leopard, perhaps? Or a wolf? Or a bull?

~ ARISTOPHANES

The fox knows many things—the hedgehog one *big* thing.

~ ARCHILOCHUS OF PAROS

Nature is to be found in her entirety nowhere more than in her smallest creatures.

~ PLINY THE ELDER

To all the rest, given (Nature) hath sufficient to clad everyone according to their kind: as namely, shells, cods, hard hides, pricks, shags, bristles, hair, down feathers, quills, scales, and fleeces of wool. The very trunks and stems of trees and plants, she hath defended with bark and rind . . . against the injuries both of heat and cold. Man alone, poor wretch, she hath laid all naked upon the earth.

~ PLINY THE ELDER

The goal of life is living in agreement with nature.

~ ZENO OF CITIUM

NECESSITY

Necessity has no law.

SAINT AUGUSTINE OF HIPPO

We give to necessity the praise of virtue.

The true creator is necessity, who is the mother of our invention.

A wise man never refuses anything to necessity.

Necessity makes even the timid brave.

Necessity, that excellent master, hath taught me many things.

PHILOSOPHY

Philosophy is the best medicine for the mind.

～ CICERO

Philosophy does not regard pedigree. She did not receive Plato as a noble, but she made him so.

～ SENECA

Let no young man delay the study of philosophy, and let no old man become weary of it, for it is never too early or too late to care for the well-being of the soul. The man who says that the season for this study has not yet come or is already past is like the man who says it is too early or too late for happiness.

～ EPICURUS

With prudence the philosopher approves or blames. If errors triumph, he departs and waits.

～ PYTHAGORAS

What is it to be a philosopher? Is it not to be prepared against events?

～ EPICTETUS

Philosophy, the love of wisdom, is impossible for the multitude.

                                      ∼ PLATO

Never proclaim yourself a philosopher nor make much talk among the ignorant about your principles, but show them by actions. Thus, at an entertainment, do not discourse how people ought to eat, but eat as you ought.

                            ∼ EPICTETUS

Socrates became perfect, improving himself by everything, following reason alone. And though you are not yet a Socrates, you ought, however, to live as one seeking to be a Socrates.

                            ∼ EPICTETUS

Of what use is a philosopher who doesn't hurt anybody's feelings?

                     ∼ DIOGENES OF SINOPE

My advice to you is to get married. If you find a good wife, you'll be happy. If not, you'll become a philosopher.

                               ∼ SOCRATES

PROCRASTINATION

Do not put your work off till tomorrow and the day after, for a sluggish worker does not fill his barn, nor one who puts off his work. Industry makes work go well, but a man who puts off work is always at hand-grips with ruin.

~ HESIOD

The rigorous are no better than the lazy during one half of life, for all men are alike when asleep.

~ ARISTOTLE

The hour is ripe, and yonder lies the way.

~ VIRGIL

Delay not to seize the hour!

~ AESCHYLUS

If you want to do something, do it!

~ PLAUTUS

The opportunity is often lost by deliberating.

~ PUBLILIUS SYRUS

If a man would move the world, he must first move himself.

~ SOCRATES

READING AND WRITING

Employ your time in improving yourself by other men's writing, so that you shall come easily by what others have labored hard for.

~ SOCRATES

The reading which has pleased, will please when repeated ten times.

~ HORACE

We must form our minds by reading deep rather than wide.

~ QUINTILIAN

He writes nothing whose readings are not read.

~ MARTIAL

Often you must turn your stylus to erase, if you hope to write anything worth a second reading.

~ HORACE

Too much polishing weakens rather than improves a work.

~ PLINY THE YOUNGER

The secret of all writing is sound judgment.

~ HORACE

To write well, express yourself like the common people but think like a wise man.

~ ARISTOTLE

REASON

The gods plant reason in mankind, of all good gifts the greatest.

~ SOPHOCLES

Reason is a light that God has kindled in the soul.

~ ARISTOTLE

The soul of man is divided into three parts: intelligence, reason, and passion. Intelligence and passion are possessed by other animals, but reason by man alone.

~ PYTHAGORAS

As far as you are able, join faith to reason.

~ BOETHIUS

Reason can in general do more than blind force.

~ GALLUS

Make reason thy guide.

~ SOLON

Reason is the ruler and queen of all things.

~ CICERO

Time heals what reason cannot.

~ SENECA

Reason is God's crowning gift to man.

~ SOPHOCLES

Reason can wrestle and overthrow terror.

~ EURIPIDES

If the work of God could be comprehended by reason, it would be no longer wonderful, and faith would have no merit if reason provided truth.

~ GREGORY I, THE GREAT

The unexamined life is not worth living.

~ SOCRATES

He who can properly summarize many ideas in a brief statement is a wise man.

~ EURIPIDES

SELF-DISCIPLINE

If men live decently, it is because discipline saves their very lives for them.

~ SOPHOCLES

Do not consider painful what is good for you.

~ EURIPIDES

When things are steep, remember to stay level-headed.

~ HORACE

What it lies within our power to do, it lies within our power not to do.

~ ARISTOTLE

You may always be victorious if you will never enter into any contest where the issue does not depend wholly upon yourself.

~ EPICTETUS

The gods help those that help themselves.

~ AESOP

SERENITY

Do not ask to have everything that happens happen as
you wish, but wish for everything to happen as it actually
does happen, and your life will be serene.

~ EPICTETUS

The first rule is to keep an untroubled spirit. The
second is to look things in the face and know them for
what they are.

~ MARCUS AURELIUS

The mind is never right but when it is at peace with
itself.

~ SENECA

He who is of a calm and happy nature will hardly feel
the pressure of age.

~ PLATO

Order your soul; reduce your wants; live in charity;
associate in Christian community; obey the laws; trust in
Providence.

~ SAINT AUGUSTINE OF HIPPO

No place can man find a quieter or more untroubled retreat than in his own soul.

                          ∽ MARCUS AURELIUS

He who has calmly reconciled his life to fate . . . can look fortune in the face.

                                      ∽ BOETHIUS

SOUL

Despise the flesh, for it passes away. Be solicitous for your soul, which will never die.

~ BASIL THE GREAT

Of all the things which a man has, next to the gods, his soul is the most divine and most truly his own.

~ PLATO

The soul is unwillingly deprived of truth.

~ EPICTETUS

When I reflect on the nature of the soul, it seems to me by far more difficult and obscure to determine its character while it is in the body, a strange domicile, than to imagine what it is when it leaves it and has arrived in the empyreal regions, in its own and proper home.

~ CICERO

The soul is the captain and ruler of the life of mortals.

~ SALLUST

The soul of man is immortal and imperishable.

∼ PLATO

The bounds of the soul thou shalt not find, though you travel every way.

∼ HERACLITUS

SPEAKING

It's a terrible thing to speak well and be wrong.

~ SOPHOCLES

Let thy speech be better than silence, or be silent.

~ DIONYSIUS THE ELDER

Speech is the mirror of the soul. As a man speaks, so is he.

~ PUBLILIUS SYRUS

It is easy to utter what has been kept silent, but impossible to recall what has been uttered.

~ PLUTARCH

First learn the meaning of what you say, and then speak.

~ EPICTETUS

By persuading others, we persuade ourselves.

~ JUNIUS

The eleventh step of humility is to speak with few and sensible words. We are to speak gently and not with a loud voice. Again, the Scriptures teach us, "The wise man is known by the fewness of his words."

∾ SAINT BENEDICT OF NURSIA

Speech is the mirror of action.

∾ SOLON

Nothing is so unbelievable that oratory cannot make it acceptable.

∾ CICERO

Grasp the subject; the words will follow.

∾ CATO THE ELDER

TRUTH

Every truth has two sides. It is well to look at *both* before we commit ourselves to either.

~ AESOP

Unless you expect the unexpected you will never find (truth), for it is hard to discover and hard to attain.

~ HERACLITUS

Truth's open to everyone, and the claims aren't all staked yet.

~ SENECA

It would be wrong to put friendship before the truth.

~ ARISTOTLE

So little trouble do men take in the search after truth; so readily do they accept whatever comes first to hand.

~ THUCYDIDES

Nowadays, flattery wins friends, truth hatred.

~ TERENCE

Why do we not hear the truth? Because we do not
speak it.

∼ PUBLILIUS SYRUS

We believe that there is no body of philosophers
however wrong, no individual however stupid, who has
not had at least a glimpse of the truth.

∼ LACTANTIUS

I am bound to tell what I am told, but not in every case
to believe it.

∼ HERODOTUS

To be absolutely sure of the truth of matters
concerning which there are many opinions is an attribute
of God not given to humans.

∼ PLATO

Truth is often eclipsed but never extinguished.

∼ LIVY

If you will be persuaded by me, pay little attention to
Sophocles, but much more to the truth, and if I appear to
you to say anything true, assent to it, but if not, oppose
me with all your might, taking good care that in my zeal I
do not deceive both myself and you and like a bee depart,
leaving my sting behind.

∼ SOPHOCLES

If any man can convince me and bring home to me
that I do not think or act aright, gladly will I change, for I
search after truth, by which man never yet was harmed.
But he is harmed who abideth still in his deception and
ignorance.

∼ MARCUS AURELIUS

None loves the messenger who brings bad news.

∾ SOPHOCLES

Throughout your life choose truth, and your words will be more believable than other people's oaths.

∾ ISOCRATES

A liar will not be believed, even when he speaks the truth.

∾ AESOP

Truth is confirmed by inspection and delay, falsehood by haste and uncertainty.

∾ PUBLILIUS SYRUS

WAR AND PEACE

We make war that we may live in peace.

~ ARISTOTLE

Be convinced that to be happy means to be free and that to be free means to be brave. Therefore do not take lightly the perils of war.

~ THUCYDIDES

Let who will boast their courage in the field; I find but little safety from my shield.

~ ARCHILOCUS OF PAROS

He who desires peace should prepare for war. He who aspires to victory should spare no pains to form his soldiers. And he who hopes for success should fight on principle, not chance.

~ VEGETIUS

Fighting men are the city's fortress.

~ ALCAEUS

Peace is liberty in tranquility.

~ CICERO

Certain peace is better than anticipated victory.

~ LIVY

War is a matter not so much of arms as of expenditure, through which arms may be made of service.

~ THUCYDIDES

Laws are silent in time of war.

~ CICERO

It is not right to exult over slain men.

~ HOMER

In peace sons bury fathers, but war violates the order of nature, and fathers bury sons.

~ HERODOTUS

It is always easy to begin a war, but very difficult to stop one.

~ SALLUST

It is not the object of war to annihilate those who have given provocation for it, but to cause them to mend their ways. Not to ruin the innocent and guilty alike, but to save both.

~ POLYBIUS

I came, I saw, I conquered.
        ~ JULIUS CAESAR (after victory at Zela in 46 B.C.)

How mad it is to summon grim death by means of war!
        ~ TIBULLUS

War should be undertaken in such a way as to show that its only object is peace.

~ CICERO

Of war, men ask the outcome but not the cause.

∾ SENECA

The only excuse for war is that we may live in peace
unharmed.

∾ CICERO

War is the last of all things to go according to schedule.

∾ THUCYDIDES

The objects at stake in a war against the barbarians are
nothing less than our country, our life, our habits, our
freedom, and all such blessings.

∾ DEMOSTHENES

You can be invincible if you never enter a contest in
which victory is not under your control.

∾ EPICTETUS

Dead men have no victory.

∾ EURIPIDES

In a just cause, the weak o'ercome the strong.

∾ SOPHOCLES

It is expedient for the victor to wish for peace restored.
For the vanquished, it is necessary.

∾ SENECA

Peace with justice and honor is the fairest and most
profitable of possessions, but with disgrace and cowardice
it is the most infamous and harmful of all.

∾ POLYBIUS

According to some accounts, when one of his men
rejoiced at the victory they had won, Pyrrhus gave this

answer: "If we win another of this cost, we are utterly
undone."

∾ PLUTARCH

Those who plot the destruction of others often perish
in the attempt.

∾ PERIANDER

Fair peace is becoming to men; fierce anger belongs to
beasts.

∾ OVID

WISDOM

Consider the little mouse, how sagacious an animal it is which never entrusts its life to one hole only.

~ PLAUTUS

From the errors of others, the wise man corrects his own.

~ PUBLILIUS SYRUS

Wisdom comes only through suffering.

~ AESCHYLUS

The function of wisdom is to discriminate between good and evil.

~ CICERO

How prone to doubt, how cautious are the wise!

~ HOMER

Those who are held wise among men, and who search for the reason of things, are those who bring the most sorrow among themselves.

~ EURIPIDES

Wisdom outweighs any wealth.

~ SOPHOCLES

Better be wise by the misfortunes of others than by
your own.

~ AESOP

Knowing what is right does not make a sagacious man.
~ ARISTOTLE

Wisdom is the highest virtue, and it has in it four other
virtues; of which one is prudence, another temperance,
the third fortitude, the fourth justice.

~ BOETHIUS

We maintain that human wisdom is a means of
education for the soul, divine wisdom being the
ultimate end.

~ ORIGEN

The virtue of wisdom more than anything else contains
a divine element which always remains.

~ PLATO

It is a profitable thing, if one is wise, to seem foolish.
~ AESCHYLUS

We Athenians, instead of looking on discussion as a
stumbling block in the way of action, think of it as an
indispensable preliminary to any wise action at all.

~ PERICLES

Wise men learn more from fools than fools from
wise men.

~ CATO THE ELDER

There is often wisdom under a shabby cloak.
~ STATIUS (also attributed to CICERO)

A short saying oft contains much wisdom.

~ SOPHOCLES

Of all our possessions, wisdom alone is immortal.

~ ISOCRATES

No man ever became wise by chance.

~ SENECA

The wise learn many things from their enemies.

ARISTOPHANES

Abundance of knowledge does not teach a man to be
wise . . . Men who love wisdom should acquaint
themselves with a great many particulars.

~ HERACLITUS

Among mortals, second thoughts are wisest.

~ EURIPIDES

He is a wise man who does not grieve for the thiings
which he has not, but rejoices for those which he has.

~ EPICTETUS

Though a man be wise, it is no shame for him to live
and learn.

~ SOPHOCLES

Wisdom is always an overmatch for strength.

~ PHAEDRUS

It takes a wise man to recognize a wise man.

~ XENOPHANES

THEY SAID IT

Great Minds among the Greeks and Romans . . .
and other prominent thinkers of the Classical age

AESCHYLUS (fifth century B.C.), *ES-kih-lus* Greek dramatist, prizewinner at Athens competitions

AESOP (sixth century B.C.), *EE-sop* Greek fabulist, reputed to have been born a slave

AGATHON (fifth century B.C.), *AG-uh-thawn* Athenian poet, friend of Plato and Euripides

AGESILAUS II (circa 444–360 B.C.), *ah-JEEZ-uh-lus* Spartan king and noted army commander

ALCAEUS (sixth century B.C.), *al-SEE-us* Greek poet

ALEXANDER THE GREAT (fourth century B.C.), *al-eg-ZAN-dur* King of Macedonia, one of the world's greatest conquerors

AMBROSE, Saint (fourth century), *AM-brohz* Bishop of Milan and writer of hymns who baptized Saint Augustine of Hippo

ANAXAGORAS (fifth century B.C.), *an-ak-SAG-ur-us* Greek philosopher

ANTISTHENES (circa 445–365 B.C.), *an-TIS-thuh-neez* Greek philosopher; founder of Cynic school of philosophy

APULEIUS, Lucius (second century), *ap-yoo-LEE-us*
Latin philosopher and satirist

ARCHILOCHUS OF PAROS (circa 714–676 B.C.), *ar-
KIL-oh-kus* Greek poet and writer of lampoons

ARCHIMEDES (third century B.C.), *ar-kih-MEE-deez*
Greek mathematician, physicist, and inventor

ARISTOPHANES (circa 450–388 B.C.), *a-ris-TOF-uh-
neez* Greek comic playwright

ARISTOTLE (384–322 B.C.), *AR-is-tah-tul* Leading
Greek philosopher, founder of the Lyceum

AUGUSTINE OF HIPPO, Saint (354–430), *AW-guh-
steen* Bishop of Hippo, theologian and philosopher,
widely regarded as the leading thinker of Christian
antiquity

AUGUSTUS CAESAR, Octavian (63 B.C.–14 A.D.), *aw-
GUS-tus* First Roman emperor, adoptive son and
heir of Julius Caesar

AUSONIUS, Declus Magnus (fourth century), *aw-
SOHN-ih-yus* Latin poet and rhetorician

BASIL THE GREAT, Saint (circa 329–379), *BAYZ-uhl*
Greek theologian and writer, bishop of Caesarea

BENEDICT OF NURSIA, Saint (circa 480–547), *BEN-
uh-dikt* Roman religious leader, founder of Western
monachism

BOETHIUS (circa 480–524), *boh-EE-thee-us* Roman philosopher, translator

CAESAR, Julius (100–44 B.C.), *SEE-zur* Roman general, charismatic statesman, political leader, and historian

CATO THE ELDER (234–149 B.C.), *KAY-toh* Roman writer, politician, and orator; author of the first manual on farming written in Latin

CATULLUS, Gaius Valerius (first century B.C.), *kuh-TUL-us* Roman lyric poet

CHRYSOSTOM, Saint John (circa 345–407), *krih-SAHS-tum* Patriarch of Constantinople; son of a wealthy Roman general, he rejected a law career for preaching

CICERO, Marcus Tullius (106–43 B.C.), *SIS-uh-roh* Roman statesman, orator, philosopher, and writer highly influential in his time

CLAUDIAN (fourth century), *KLAW-dih-un* Last of the great Latin poets

CLEMENT OF ALEXANDRIA, Saint (circa 150–215), *KLEM-ent* Theologian, head of the catechetical school at Alexandria

CLEOBULUS (sixth century B.C.), *klee-OH-buh-lus* Greek poet-philosopher

CLIMACUS, Saint John (circa 579–649), *klih-MAK-us* Abbot of the monastery on Mount Sinai and influential Christian ascetical writer

Bill Bradfield

CYPRIAN, Saint (circa 200–258), *SIP-ree-an* Bishop at Carthage who suffered martyrdom

DEMETRIUS (circa 345–283 B.C.), *duh-MEE-tree-us* Greek orator and statesman

DEMOCRITUS (circa 460–370 B.C.), *dih-MAH-kruh-tus* Greek philosopher

DEMOSTHENES (circa 383–322 B.C.), *dih-MOS-theh-neez* Greek constitutional lawyer, politician, and orator

DIODORUS SICULUS (first century B.C.), *dye-uh-DOH-rus SIK-uh-lus* Roman author who wrote an immense history of the world, the forty-volume *Bibliotheke Historike*

DIOGENES OF SINOPE (fourth century B.C.), *dye-AHJ-uh-neez* Greek philosopher, ascetic and moralist who, with Antisthenes, founded the Cynic sect

DIONYSIUS THE ELDER (430–367 B.C.), *dye-uh-NISH-ee-us* Greek poet who became absolute ruler of Syracuse and warred with Carthaginians and other enemies

ENNIUS, Quintus (239–169 B.C.), *en-NEE-yus* Early Roman poet, well-known for his tragedies based on Greek drama

EPICTETUS (50–130), *eh-pik-TAY-tus* Greek philosopher, prolific writer of maxims

EPICURUS (341–270 B.C.), *eh-pih-KYOOR-us* Greek philosopher, founder of two schools

EUCLID (325–265 B.C.), *YOO-klid* Greek
mathematician and teacher

EUDOXUS OF CNIDUS (fourth century B.C.), *yoo-
DOKS-us* Greek astronomer and geometer

EURIPIDES (fifth century B.C.), *yoo-RIP-ih-deez* Greek
playwright, author of more than eighty dramas

GALLUS, Cornelius (first century B.C.), *GAHL-us*
Roman poet noted for four books of elegies

GELLIUS, Aulus (second century), *JEL-yus* Scholar,
author, and grammarian; judicial authority at Rome

GREGORY I, THE GREAT (540–602), *GREG-oh-ree*
Pope and saint who created papal system lasting
through the Middle Ages

HERACLITUS (circa 540–480 B.C.), *her-uh-KLYE-tus*
Greek philosopher noted for innate pessimism

HERODOTUS (fifth century B.C.), *hih-ROD-uh-tus*
Greek historian; author of history of the Greco-
Persian wars from 500 to 479 B.C.

HESIOD (circa 800 B.C.), *HEE-see-ud* Greek poet and
historian

HIPPOCRATES (circa 460–377 B.C.), *hih-PAH-kruh-teez*
Greek physician who devised code of medical ethics

HIPPOLYTUS, Saint (170–235), *hih-POL-ih-tus* Greek
theological writer, a presbyter at Rome

HOMER (eighth century B.C.), *HOH-mer* Greek poet to whom authorship of two epic works—the *Iliad* and the *Odyssey*—is ascribed

HORACE (first century B.C.), *HAWR-us* Roman poet laureate and satirist, a master of the common range of thought and feeling

HYPATIA OF ALEXANDRIA (circa 375–415), *hye-PAY-shuh* Astronomer, mathematician, and lecturer; first notable woman in field of mathematics

ISOCRATES (circa 436–338 B.C.), *ih-SAH-kruh-teez* Roman orator, founder of a school in Athens

JEROME, Saint (circa 342–420), *juh-ROHM* Christian ascetic, scholar, and writer

JULIUS CAESAR—see Caesar, Julius

JUSTINIAN I (circa 482–565), *juh-STIN-ee-un* Roman emperor whose rule began in 527

JUVENAL (circa 60–130), *JOO-vuh-nul* Roman poet, a satirist who exposed society's decadence under Emperor Domitian

LACTANTIUS, Lucius (fourth century), *lak-TANSH-us* Christian apologist and rhetorician chosen by Constantine as a tutor to his son, Crispus

LIVY, Titus (circa 59 B.C.–17 A.D.), *LIH-vee* Roman writer, aide to Emperor Augustus; author of the 142-volume *History of Rome*

LONGINUS, Cassius (circa 213–273), *lahn-JYE-nus*
Greek rhetorician and critic-philosopher who taught
in Athens for forty years

LUCAN (circa 39–65), *LOO-kun* Latin poet born in
Spain, briefly a friend of Nero; his work became
popular in the Middle Ages

LUCRETIUS (first century B.C.), *LOO-kree-shus* Latin
writer and philosopher, known for his one long poem
On the Nature of Things

LYCOPHRON OF CHALCIS (third century B.C.), *LYE-
koh-frahn* Greek scholar and poet

MARCUS AURELIUS (121–180), *MAHR-kus aw-REEL-
yus* Roman emperor and eminent Stoic philosopher
who wrote *Meditations* as precepts of practical
morality

MARTIAL, Marcus Valerius (circa 38–103), *MAHR-shul*
Roman epigrammatic poet and military tribune

MENANDER (circa 343–292 B.C.), *muh-NAN-der* Greek
playwright, author of more than 100 comedies

MIMNERMUS OF COLOPHON (seventh century B.C.),
mim-NUR-mus Greek elegiac poet

ORIGEN (185–254), *AWR-uh-jen* Eclectic Greek writer
who produced great theological works including
textual studies on the Old Testament

OVID (43 B.C.–17 A.D.), *AH-vud* Voluminous Latin poet,
remembered partly for his versatility and frivolity

PAPPUS OF ALEXANDRIA (fourth century), *PAP-us* Greek mathematician and writer

PARMENIDES (fifth century B.C.), *pahr-MEH-nih-deez* Greek Presocratic philosopher, greatest of the Eleatic school

PERIANDER (circa 665–585 B.C.), *per-ih-AN-der* One of the "Seven Wise Men of Greece," he became the second absolute ruler of Corinth

PERICLES (fifth century B.C.), *PEH-ruh-kleez* Athenian naval commander and statesman who led rebuilding of Athens after the Persian Wars

PETRONIUS, Gaius (first century), *pih-TROH-nee-us* Latin writer believed to be the author of *Satirae*, a satirical verse-and-prose romance

PHAEDRUS (first century), *FEE-druhs* Translator of Aesop's fables into Latin verse

PHILOLAUS OF CROTON (fifth century B.C.), *fil-oh-LAY-us* Greek Pythagorean philosopher

PINDAR (circa 522–480 B.C.), *PIN-dahr* Greek lyric poet

PITTACUS OF MITYLENE (circa 650–570 B.C.), *PIT-a-kus* One of the "Seven Wise Men of Greece," and ruler of Mitylene

PLATO (circa 427–347 B.C.), *PLAY-toh* Greek genius who, with Aristotle and Socrates, laid philosophical foundations of Western culture

PLAUTUS (circa 254–184 B.C.), *PLOH-tus* Rome's chief comic poet, also a dramatist

PLINY THE ELDER (23–79), *PLIN-ih* Prodigious Roman author of works on military tactics, natural science, history, other topics

PLINY THE YOUNGER (61–113), *PLIN-ih* Successor to his uncle as a prominent Roman literary figure; scientist and author of nine books

PLOTINUS (circa 205–270), *ploh-TIH-nus* Egypt-born Roman philosopher, chief advocate of Neoplatonist ideas

PLUTARCH (circa 46–121), *PLOO-tahrk* Greek biographer, historian, and philosopher

POLYBIUS (second century B.C.), *puh-LIB-ee-us* Roman historian

POLYCARP, Saint (circa 70–158), *PAH-lih-karp* Influential bishop of Smyrna; burned at stake during persecution of Christians

PRISCIAN (sixth century), *PRISH-an* Latin grammarian, teacher at Constantinople

PROCLUS (circa 410–485), *PROH-klus* Greek philosopher and vigorous defender of paganism

PUBLILIUS SYRUS (first century B.C.), *pub-LIL-ih-us SYE-rus* Author of Latin mimes in which he became an improvisational actor; also, a prolific writer of wise and witty maxims

PYTHAGORAS (sixth century B.C.), *puh-THAG-uh-rus* Greek geometer and philosopher

QUINTILIAN (first century), *kwin-TIL-yun* Roman orator, author of a book on rhetoric

SALLUST (first century B.C.), *SAL-ust* Roman historian and senator

SAPPHO OF LESBOS (seventh century B.C.), *SAF-oh* Greek poetess, writer of passionate and intimate lyrics

SENECA, Marcus Annaeus (circa 55 B.C.–40 A.D.), *SEN-ih-kah* Roman provincial officer, historian, and rhetorician born in Cordova, Spain. Called "the Elder"

SENECA, Lucius Annaeus (circa 4 B.C.–65 A.D.), *SEN-ih-kah* Playwright, essayist, philosopher, statesman, and Rome's leading intellectual figure of his time

SIMONIDES OF CEOS (556–468 B.C.), *sye-MOHN-ih-deez* Greek lyric poet, writer of epigrams, elegies, odes, and dirges about heroic soldiers

SOCRATES (circa 469–399 B.C.), *SOK-ruh-teez* Greek philosopher whom the Delphic Oracle called "the wisest man in the world"

SOLON (circa 638–559 B.C.), *SOH-lun* One of the nine principal magistrates of Athens; a constitutional reformer, poet, and merchant

SOPHOCLES (fifth century B.C.), *SOF-uh-kleez* Greek author wrote 122 plays, of which seven survive, including *Oedipus Rex*, called the true masterpiece of classical drama

STATIUS (circa 45–96), *STAY-shee-us* Latin poet, born at Naples

STESICHORUS (circa 640–555 B.C.), *stay-SIK-oh-rus* Greek lyric poet, legendary inventor of the choral "heroic hymn"

SUETONIUS (75–160), *SWEE-toh-nee-us* Roman biographer and antiquarian

TACITUS (circa 55–120), *TAS-ih-toos* Roman lawyer and historian

TERENCE (circa 190–59 B.C.), *TEHR-uns* Roman author of comedies

TERENTIANUS MAURUS (second century), *teh-ren-shih-AY-nus MAH-rus* Roman author who wrote hexameter treatise on prosody, comprising four books

TERTULLIAN, Quintus Septimus (circa 160–220), *tur-TOOL-yun* Roman theologian, one of the Carthaginian fathers of the Latin church

THALES (sixth century B.C.), *THAY-leez* Greek philosopher of the Ionian school, said to have invented geometry by deductive reasoning

THEOCRITUS (third century B.C.), *thee-OCK-rih-tus* Greek pastoral poet

THEOGNIS (570–490 B.C.), *thee-OG-nis* Greek elegiac poet

THEOPHRASTUS (circa 372–286 B.C.), *thee-of-FRAS-tus* Greek philosopher, inheritor of Aristotle's library

THUCYDIDES (fifth century B.C.), *THOO-sid-i-deez* Greek historian of the Peloponnesian war

TIBULLUS, Albius (first century B.C.), *tuh-BUHL-uhs* Roman elegiac poet

VEGETIUS (fourth century), *veh-JEE-shus* Roman author whose writings on warfare became a classic study during the Middle Ages

VIRGIL, *also* VERGIL (70–19 B.C.), *VUR-juhl* Greatest of the Latin poets

XENOPHANES (circa 580–470 B.C.), *zuh-NOF-uh-neez* Greek philosopher

XENOPHON (circa 431–342 B.C.), *ZEHN-uh-fun* Greek historian

ZENO OF CITIUM (circa 342–270 B.C.), *ZEE-noh* Founder of Stoic philosophy who established his school at the "Painted Porch" in Athens and wrote 18 books

ZENO OF ELEA (fifth century B.C.), *ZEE-noh* Greek philosopher and mathematician

A CATALOG OF SELECTED
DOVER BOOKS
IN ALL FIELDS OF INTEREST

A CATALOG OF SELECTED DOVER
BOOKS IN ALL FIELDS OF INTEREST

100 BEST-LOVED POEMS, Edited by Philip Smith. "The Passionate Shepherd to His Love," "Shall I compare thee to a summer's day?" "Death, be not proud," "The Raven," "The Road Not Taken," plus works by Blake, Wordsworth, Byron, Shelley, Keats, many others. 96pp. 5³⁄₁₆ x 8¼.   0-486-28553-7

100 SMALL HOUSES OF THE THIRTIES, Brown-Blodgett Company. Exterior photographs and floor plans for 100 charming structures. Illustrations of models accompanied by descriptions of interiors, color schemes, closet space, and other amenities. 200 illustrations. 112pp. 8⅜ x 11.   0-486-44131-8

1000 TURN-OF-THE-CENTURY HOUSES: With Illustrations and Floor Plans, Herbert C. Chivers. Reproduced from a rare edition, this showcase of homes ranges from cottages and bungalows to sprawling mansions. Each house is meticulously illustrated and accompanied by complete floor plans. 256pp. 9⅜ x 12¼.

0-486-45596-3

101 GREAT AMERICAN POEMS, Edited by The American Poetry & Literacy Project. Rich treasury of verse from the 19th and 20th centuries includes works by Edgar Allan Poe, Robert Frost, Walt Whitman, Langston Hughes, Emily Dickinson, T. S. Eliot, other notables. 96pp. 5³⁄₁₆ x 8¼.   0-486-40158-8

101 GREAT SAMURAI PRINTS, Utagawa Kuniyoshi. Kuniyoshi was a master of the warrior woodblock print — and these 18th-century illustrations represent the pinnacle of his craft. Full-color portraits of renowned Japanese samurais pulse with movement, passion, and remarkably fine detail. 112pp. 8⅜ x 11.   0-486-46523-3

ABC OF BALLET, Janet Grosser. Clearly worded, abundantly illustrated little guide defines basic ballet-related terms: arabesque, battement, pas de chat, relevé, sissonne, many others. Pronunciation guide included. Excellent primer. 48pp. 4³⁄₁₆ x 5¾.

0-486-40871-X

ACCESSORIES OF DRESS: An Illustrated Encyclopedia, Katherine Lester and Bess Viola Oerke. Illustrations of hats, veils, wigs, cravats, shawls, shoes, gloves, and other accessories enhance an engaging commentary that reveals the humor and charm of the many-sided story of accessorized apparel. 644 figures and 59 plates. 608pp. 6 ⅛ x 9¼.

0-486-43378-1

ADVENTURES OF HUCKLEBERRY FINN, Mark Twain. Join Huck and Jim as their boyhood adventures along the Mississippi River lead them into a world of excitement, danger, and self-discovery. Humorous narrative, lyrical descriptions of the Mississippi valley, and memorable characters. 224pp. 5³⁄₁₆ x 8¼.   0-486-28061-6

ALICE STARMORE'S BOOK OF FAIR ISLE KNITTING, Alice Starmore. A noted designer from the region of Scotland's Fair Isle explores the history and techniques of this distinctive, stranded-color knitting style and provides copious illustrated instructions for 14 original knitwear designs. 208pp. 8⅜ x 10⅞.   0-486-47218-3

Browse over 9,000 books at www.doverpublications.com

ALICE'S ADVENTURES IN WONDERLAND, Lewis Carroll. Beloved classic about a little girl lost in a topsy-turvy land and her encounters with the White Rabbit, March Hare, Mad Hatter, Cheshire Cat, and other delightfully improbable characters. 42 illustrations by Sir John Tenniel. 96pp. 5³⁄₁₆ x 8¼. 0-486-27543-4

AMERICA'S LIGHTHOUSES: An Illustrated History, Francis Ross Holland. Profusely illustrated fact-filled survey of American lighthouses since 1716. Over 200 stations — East, Gulf, and West coasts, Great Lakes, Hawaii, Alaska, Puerto Rico, the Virgin Islands, and the Mississippi and St. Lawrence Rivers. 240pp. 8 x 10¾.
0-486-25576-X

AN ENCYCLOPEDIA OF THE VIOLIN, Alberto Bachmann. Translated by Frederick H. Martens. Introduction by Eugene Ysaye. First published in 1925, this renowned reference remains unsurpassed as a source of essential information, from construction and evolution to repertoire and technique. Includes a glossary and 73 illustrations. 496pp. 6⅛ x 9¼. 0-486-46618-3

ANIMALS: 1,419 Copyright-Free Illustrations of Mammals, Birds, Fish, Insects, etc., Selected by Jim Harter. Selected for its visual impact and ease of use, this outstanding collection of wood engravings presents over 1,000 species of animals in extremely lifelike poses. Includes mammals, birds, reptiles, amphibians, fish, insects, and other invertebrates. 284pp. 9 x 12. 0-486-23766-4

THE ANNALS, Tacitus. Translated by Alfred John Church and William Jackson Brodribb. This vital chronicle of Imperial Rome, written by the era's great historian, spans A.D. 14-68 and paints incisive psychological portraits of major figures, from Tiberius to Nero. 416pp. 5³⁄₁₆ x 8¼. 0-486-45236-0

ANTIGONE, Sophocles. Filled with passionate speeches and sensitive probing of moral and philosophical issues, this powerful and often-performed Greek drama reveals the grim fate that befalls the children of Oedipus. Footnotes. 64pp. 5³⁄₁₆ x 8 ¼. 0-486-27804-2

ART DECO DECORATIVE PATTERNS IN FULL COLOR, Christian Stoll. Reprinted from a rare 1910 portfolio, 160 sensuous and exotic images depict a breathtaking array of florals, geometrics, and abstracts — all elegant in their stark simplicity. 64pp. 8⅜ x 11. 0-486-44862-2

THE ARTHUR RACKHAM TREASURY: 86 Full-Color Illustrations, Arthur Rackham. Selected and Edited by Jeff A. Menges. A stunning treasury of 86 full-page plates span the famed English artist's career, from *Rip Van Winkle* (1905) to masterworks such as *Undine, A Midsummer Night's Dream,* and *Wind in the Willows* (1939). 96pp. 8⅜ x 11.
0-486-44685-9

THE AUTHENTIC GILBERT & SULLIVAN SONGBOOK, W. S. Gilbert and A. S. Sullivan. The most comprehensive collection available, this songbook includes selections from every one of Gilbert and Sullivan's light operas. Ninety-two numbers are presented uncut and unedited, and in their original keys. 410pp. 9 x 12.
0-486-23482-7

THE AWAKENING, Kate Chopin. First published in 1899, this controversial novel of a New Orleans wife's search for love outside a stifling marriage shocked readers. Today, it remains a first-rate narrative with superb characterization. New introductory Note. 128pp. 5³⁄₁₆ x 8¼. 0-486-27786-0

BASIC DRAWING, Louis Priscilla. Beginning with perspective, this commonsense manual progresses to the figure in movement, light and shade, anatomy, drapery, composition, trees and landscape, and outdoor sketching. Black-and-white illustrations throughout. 128pp. 8⅜ x 11. 0-486-45815-6

THE BATTLES THAT CHANGED HISTORY, Fletcher Pratt. Historian profiles 16 crucial conflicts, ancient to modern, that changed the course of Western civilization. Gripping accounts of battles led by Alexander the Great, Joan of Arc, Ulysses S. Grant, other commanders. 27 maps. 352pp. 5⅜ x 8½.   0-486-41129-X

BEETHOVEN'S LETTERS, Ludwig van Beethoven. Edited by Dr. A. C. Kalischer. Features 457 letters to fellow musicians, friends, greats, patrons, and literary men. Reveals musical thoughts, quirks of personality, insights, and daily events. Includes 15 plates. 410pp. 5⅜ x 8½.   0-486-22769-3

BERNICE BOBS HER HAIR AND OTHER STORIES, F. Scott Fitzgerald. This brilliant anthology includes 6 of Fitzgerald's most popular stories: "The Diamond as Big as the Ritz," the title tale, "The Offshore Pirate," "The Ice Palace," "The Jelly Bean," and "May Day." 176pp. 5⅜ x 8½.   0-486-47049-0

BESLER'S BOOK OF FLOWERS AND PLANTS: 73 Full-Color Plates from Hortus Eystettensis, 1613, Basilius Besler. Here is a selection of magnificent plates from the *Hortus Eystettensis,* which vividly illustrated and identified the plants, flowers, and trees that thrived in the legendary German garden at Eichstätt. 80pp. 8⅜ x 11.
0-486-46005-3

THE BOOK OF KELLS, Edited by Blanche Cirker. Painstakingly reproduced from a rare facsimile edition, this volume contains full-page decorations, portraits, illustrations, plus a sampling of textual leaves with exquisite calligraphy and ornamentation. 32 full-color illustrations. 32pp. 9⅜ x 12¼.   0-486-24345-1

THE BOOK OF THE CROSSBOW: With an Additional Section on Catapults and Other Siege Engines, Ralph Payne-Gallwey. Fascinating study traces history and use of crossbow as military and sporting weapon, from Middle Ages to modern times. Also covers related weapons: balistas, catapults, Turkish bows, more. Over 240 illustrations. 400pp. 7¼ x 10⅛.   0-486-28720-3

THE BUNGALOW BOOK: Floor Plans and Photos of 112 Houses, 1910, Henry L. Wilson. Here are 112 of the most popular and economic blueprints of the early 20th century — plus an illustration or photograph of each completed house. A wonderful time capsule that still offers a wealth of valuable insights. 160pp. 8⅜ x 11.
0-486-45104-6

THE CALL OF THE WILD, Jack London. A classic novel of adventure, drawn from London's own experiences as a Klondike adventurer, relating the story of a heroic dog caught in the brutal life of the Alaska Gold Rush. Note. 64pp. 5³⁄₁₆ x 8¼.
0-486-26472-6

CANDIDE, Voltaire. Edited by Francois-Marie Arouet. One of the world's great satires since its first publication in 1759. Witty, caustic skewering of romance, science, philosophy, religion, government — nearly all human ideals and institutions. 112pp. 5³⁄₁₆ x 8¼.   0-486-26689-3

CELEBRATED IN THEIR TIME: Photographic Portraits from the George Grantham Bain Collection, Edited by Amy Pastan. With an Introduction by Michael Carlebach. Remarkable portrait gallery features 112 rare images of Albert Einstein, Charlie Chaplin, the Wright Brothers, Henry Ford, and other luminaries from the worlds of politics, art, entertainment, and industry. 128pp. 8⅜ x 11.   0-486-46754-6

CHARIOTS FOR APOLLO: The NASA History of Manned Lunar Spacecraft to 1969, Courtney G. Brooks, James M. Grimwood, and Loyd S. Swenson, Jr. This illustrated history by a trio of experts is the definitive reference on the Apollo spacecraft and lunar modules. It traces the vehicles' design, development, and operation in space. More than 100 photographs and illustrations. 576pp. 6¾ x 9¼. 0-486-46756-2

A CHRISTMAS CAROL, Charles Dickens. This engrossing tale relates Ebenezer Scrooge's ghostly journeys through Christmases past, present, and future and his ultimate transformation from a harsh and grasping old miser to a charitable and compassionate human being. 80pp. 5³⁄₁₆ x 8¼. 0-486-26865-9

COMMON SENSE, Thomas Paine. First published in January of 1776, this highly influential landmark document clearly and persuasively argued for American separation from Great Britain and paved the way for the Declaration of Independence. 64pp. 5³⁄₁₆ x 8¼. 0-486-29602-4

THE COMPLETE SHORT STORIES OF OSCAR WILDE, Oscar Wilde. Complete texts of "The Happy Prince and Other Tales," "A House of Pomegranates," "Lord Arthur Savile's Crime and Other Stories," "Poems in Prose," and "The Portrait of Mr. W. H." 208pp. 5³⁄₁₆ x 8¼. 0-486-45216-6

COMPLETE SONNETS, William Shakespeare. Over 150 exquisite poems deal with love, friendship, the tyranny of time, beauty's evanescence, death, and other themes in language of remarkable power, precision, and beauty. Glossary of archaic terms. 80pp. 5³⁄₁₆ x 8¼. 0-486-26686-9

THE COUNT OF MONTE CRISTO: Abridged Edition, Alexandre Dumas. Falsely accused of treason, Edmond Dantès is imprisoned in the bleak Chateau d'If. After a hair-raising escape, he launches an elaborate plot to extract a bitter revenge against those who betrayed him. 448pp. 5³⁄₁₆ x 8¼. 0-486-45643-9

CRAFTSMAN BUNGALOWS: Designs from the Pacific Northwest, Yoho & Merritt. This reprint of a rare catalog, showcasing the charming simplicity and cozy style of Craftsman bungalows, is filled with photos of completed homes, plus floor plans and estimated costs. An indispensable resource for architects, historians, and illustrators. 112pp. 10 x 7. 0-486-46875-5

CRAFTSMAN BUNGALOWS: 59 Homes from "The Craftsman," Edited by Gustav Stickley. Best and most attractive designs from Arts and Crafts Movement publication — 1903–1916 — includes sketches, photographs of homes, floor plans, descriptive text. 128pp. 8¼ x 11. 0-486-25829-7

CRIME AND PUNISHMENT, Fyodor Dostoyevsky. Translated by Constance Garnett. Supreme masterpiece tells the story of Raskolnikov, a student tormented by his own thoughts after he murders an old woman. Overwhelmed by guilt and terror, he confesses and goes to prison. 480pp. 5³⁄₁₆ x 8¼. 0-486-41587-2

THE DECLARATION OF INDEPENDENCE AND OTHER GREAT DOCUMENTS OF AMERICAN HISTORY: 1775-1865, Edited by John Grafton. Thirteen compelling and influential documents: Henry's "Give Me Liberty or Give Me Death," Declaration of Independence, The Constitution, Washington's First Inaugural Address, The Monroe Doctrine, The Emancipation Proclamation, Gettysburg Address, more. 64pp. 5³⁄₁₆ x 8¼. 0-486-41124-9

THE DESERT AND THE SOWN: Travels in Palestine and Syria, Gertrude Bell. "The female Lawrence of Arabia," Gertrude Bell wrote captivating, perceptive accounts of her travels in the Middle East. This intriguing narrative, accompanied by 160 photos, traces her 1905 sojourn in Lebanon, Syria, and Palestine. 368pp. 5⅜ x 8½. 0-486-46876-3

A DOLL'S HOUSE, Henrik Ibsen. Ibsen's best-known play displays his genius for realistic prose drama. An expression of women's rights, the play climaxes when the central character, Nora, rejects a smothering marriage and life in "a doll's house." 80pp. 5³⁄₁₆ x 8¼. 0-486-27062-9

Browse over 9,000 books at www.doverpublications.com